IMAGES OF ENGLAND

Heath Town
and Fallings Park

The centre of Heath Town in June 1969. Looking from the top of Campion House it is possible to see the crossroads where Wednesfield Road, Deans Road and Tudor Road meet, and the Heath Town railway tunnel which runs underneath. During the Second World War the factory on the right was occupied by Redwing Aircraft who made parts for Defiants and other aircraft, and is now the site of the Kwik Save supermarket.

IMAGES OF ENGLAND

Heath Town
and Fallings Park

Alec Brew

NONSUCH

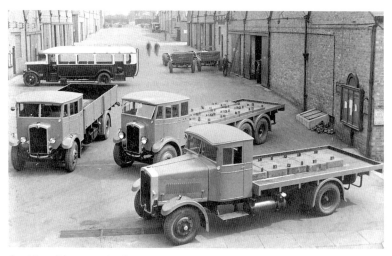

Guy Motors' factory yard, Fallings Park, with a selection of their commercial vehicles in 1930. Sidney Guy's factory opened in Park Lane in 1913 and had expanded considerably by 1930. Guy Motors was the only one of the many Wolverhampton vehicle manufacturers from this period to survive the Depression.

First published 1999
This new pocket edition 2005
Text and images unchanged from first edition

Nonsuch Publishing Limited
The Mill, Brimscombe Port,
Stroud, Gloucestershire, GL5 2QG
www.nonsuch-publishing.com

British Library Cataloguing in Publication Data.
A catalogue record for this book is available from the British Library.

ISBN 1-84588-114-1

Typesetting and origination by Nonsuch Publishing Limited
Printed in Great Britain by Oaklands Book Services Limited

Contents

Introduction   7

1.   Heath Town   9

2.   Park Village   39

3.   Springfield   49

4.   Stafford Street to Broad Street   81

5.   Fallings Park   93

6.   Wood End   121

Acknowledgements   128

Dignitaries gathered in Park Village in July 1908 to inspect a Model Housing Exhibition, part of the plan to create the garden suburb of Fallings Park.

The people of Beacon Street, Springfield, celebrate VE Day. Behind the big bass drum of Mr Helliwell is his wife wearing the long dress.

Introduction

The small township of Heath Town began life as Wednesfield Heath, an adjunct of Wednesfield, situated around the crossroads where the Wolverhampton to Wednesfield Road and the ancient road from Worcester to Stafford meet. The latter ran along the line of Deans Road, Church Road and Bushbury Road, which lay on a ridge with a good view, over the valley of Smestow Brook. The town of Wolverhampton sat on top of the nearby hill. The importance of this crossroads gives weight to Heath Town's claim to be the location of the AD 910 Battle of Woden's Field, between the Saxons and the Danes. No physical evidence of the battle site has yet been found, but claims for its location have been made from Tettenhall to Wednesfield. In actual fact the battle may have fluctuated through the woods across a large part of the area.

The tiny crossroads community that may have occupied Wednesfield Heath for the subsequent centuries was boosted by the coal-mining that gradually encompassed the whole area to the south. The Birmingham Canal navigation led to the opening of the Wyrley and Essington Canal in 1797 for the purpose of transporting coal from the Wednesfield Heath area and the Cannock coalfield. Forty years later, Wednesfield Heath boasted the first railway station in the area when the Grand Junction Railway was built to link the London and Birmingham Railway with the Liverpool and Manchester Railway. The station was named Wolverhampton until High Level Station was built some years later, after which it became Wednesfield Heath. It became a goods station in 1872 when Midland Railway's Walsall to Wolverhampton line opened, serving the new Heath Town station.

The population of Wednesfield Heath had grown to such an extent by 1850 that it was decided to split Wednesfield parish into two. Sir John Moor Paget gave land for a new church and the foundation stone for Holy Trinity was laid in the same year. The church opened on 21 July 1852, and two years later the adjacent church school and six almshouses were also built.

The two parishes still co-operated, pooling their resources on such matters as education and sewage, and in 1893 they both became Urban Districts. Heath Town existed as an independent community for thirty-four years, but in 1927 the pressure of its large, expanding neighbour to the west became overwhelming and it was absorbed into Wolverhampton. Wolverhampton had already built its large new workhouse on a site between Heath Town and Wednesfield and this has slowly developed into the vast New Cross Hospital site.

At the turn of the century the main factory in Heath Town was Joseph Evans' huge Culwell Works in Woden Road, which produced heavy duty pumps. Later, Manders' Paints and Inks came to dominate the local industrial scene. The new Chubb Lock and Safe Works on Wednesfield Road was actually built on the Wolverhampton side of the boundary, though it is now considered to be in Heath Town. When the works were built, Heath Town and the Springfield area of Wolverhampton were actually separated by the fields of Grimstone Farm, which stretched from Woden Road to Hilton Street.

As its name suggests, Springfield featured freshwater springs, and these are probably what drew William Butler to build his brewery there. The first beer from Butler's was brewed in 1874. Many of the workers who lived in the terraced streets of houses which huddled next to Springfield Brewery were employed at Butler's. Others worked on the railways that cut off Springfield from the town centre. Wolverhampton's Low Level Station lay just the other side of Wednesfield Road from Springfield, lying in the shadow of High Level Station. The shortcut to town for Springfield workers went up 'The Nineteen Steps' (though there were only ever eighteen), over the Great Western Railway footbridge, directly under the Lock Street bridge of the London and North Western Railway and over the Lock Street canal bridge. This provided a formidable series of barriers.

Beyond the railway were more rows of terraced houses clustered around a smaller brewery called Russell's. This area was bounded by Stafford Street and Broad Street. At the bottom end of Stafford Street, Cannock Road led to the lower part of Springfield via Grimstone Farm, and then to the Park Village area of Heath Town.

When a model village was instigated in 1908 by the Paget family, the area where it was constructed, around the Cannock Road and Bushbury Road junction, was surrounded by farmland. As the twentieth century progressed, the expanding urban areas of Wolverhampton on one side and Wednesfield on the other slowly engulfed Park Village, making its title something of a misnomer. The expansion was led by the industrialisation of the area around Park Lane, with large companies like Guy Motors, Henry Meadows, Efandam (later Ever Ready) and A.B. Coupler setting up in the area. After the First World War, Fallings Park became a major area of urban expansion for Wolverhampton on one side of Cannock Road, and Wednesfield underwent similar changes on the other.

The incorporation of Wednesfield into Wolverhampton in 1966 completed the process of turning the whole area into an amorphous mass of housing, with pockets of industrialisation. The housing continued to spread out to Wood End, where the expansion of Wolverhampton met the Staffordshire county boundary and the rural tranquillity beyond.

One

Heath Town

Nowadays, Heath Town is thought of as a vast 1960s housing estate built around Wednesfield Road like an island at the centre of a small Black Country township. From 1852, when it was split from Wednesfield, until 1927, when it was amalgamated with Wolverhampton, Heath Town was an independent community surrounded by green fields on three sides and the desolate coal workings of Bowman's Harbour on the other.

Heath Town suffered from having its heart destroyed when the old main shopping street along Wednesfield Road was demolished in the 1960s. Although shops were built on the new estate, no one outside the estate knew they were there and they soon closed. The centre of Heath Town is now based around Holy Trinity church and the swimming baths, but there are no shops or other services there. Heath Town was famous for its swimming baths and the giant New Cross Hospital, though in recent times it is better known as the site of Wolverhampton's first multi-screen cinema. The disused coal workings of Bowman's Harbour and beyond have finally been redeveloped for industrial and leisure purposes after more than a century of neglect.

Part of Heath Town viewed from the top of Campion House in 1968. Holy Trinity church and its graveyard containing its six almshouses are prominent. In the foreground are Heath Town baths, which were opened in 1932. Beyond is Holy Trinity school, which burned down in 1985 when it had become just an annexe to the 1970s school constructed in the fields visible on the left.

Holy Trinity church, shortly before the First World War. The foundation stone had been laid in 1850 on land given by Sir John Moor Paget, when Wednesfield Heath was split from Wednesfield parish. The church opened on 21 July 1852.

The six almshouses were built in the Holy Trinity churchyard in 1854, the same year the new Holy Trinity school opened. After being derelict for many years, the almshouses have recently been renovated by the Bromford-Carinthia Housing Association.

The centre of Heath Town, around 1905. The Wolverhampton tram is on Wednesfield Road and Railway Street is off to the left. The people in the centre are in front of a bank and the Star Hotel is on the right.

The Alma Vics football team is believed to have been based in Alma Street, Heath Town, around 1900. The man with the towel on the left is Edgar Beddard and in the middle of the back row is Sydney Beddard.

The laying of the foundation stone of the Wolverhampton Workhouse in 1900, at a site between Heath Town and Wednesfield. The huge new complex opened in 1903 and became New Cross Hospital in the 1920s.

Opposite above: Richards' Beau Ideal Cycle Company in Railway Street, Heath Town, at the turn of the century. The firm also had major showrooms in the Gresham Buildings, New Lichfield Street, Wolverhampton.

Opposite below: Local men outside the Park Inn in Cannock Road, near the end of Park Lane, before 1911. The landlord, William Whittingham, could well be the man in the doorway, while the man seated second right is Charles Woodward who worked at Stafford Road Locomotive Works. The reason for the photograph is not known, but most of the men are wearing flowers in their buttonholes, so it was obviously a special occasion.

Chubb carriages outside Woden Road school on 9 July 1908. The carriages were brought up from London to convey dignitaries from the laying of the foundation stone for the new Chubb Factory on Wednesfield Road to the Model Housing Exhibition in Park Village.

Woden Road school's Group IV photograph in 1908. The school was built in 1898 by the joint Heath Town and Wednesfield School Board, initially for 400 pupils.

Wednesfield Road, Heath Town, around the turn of the century. The Lorain system trams (surface contact) had been built by the Wolverhampton Corporation's transport department and the Wednesfield route opened as far as Church Street, Heath Town, on 22 June 1904.

The interior of the giant Joseph Evans & Sons' Culwell Works at the turn of the century. The factory made hand, steam and hydraulic pumps. The factory lay between Woden Road and the railway. The machinery, which all worked from belts operating off a single shaft, and the trucks on rails which brought the castings from the iron and brass foundries should be noted. This system remained until after the Second World War.

Powell Street is typical of the terraced streets in the Park Village area. The little white dog on the right has come out to investigate the figure (blurred) by the second lamp-post.

Outside Watkins' Bakery in Wolverhampton Road, Heath Town, around 1927. From left to right: Sam Watkins, Jack Coleman, Rachel Watkins, Arthur Watkins. Rachel Watkins would not sell cakes to anyone who did not regularly buy bread there and she would order kids with runny noses out of the shop.

Wednesfield Road, Heath Town, before the First World War. St Barnabas' church in the background is the only building that survives today as the whole area was cleared in the 1960s for the new housing estate and dual carriageway.

Heath Town United football team, around 1936. Back row, left to right: C. Courtney, M. Hodgkins, W. Wardle, J. Eaton. Middle row: R. Rushton, J. Weaver, F. Tranter J. Wright, A. Ward, F. Middleton, S. Lloyd, D. Tranter, N. Williams. Front row: B. Brown, F. Bullock, wL. Stallard, D. Courtney, H. Walters, F. Bibb, H. Reay. In front: J. Rushton.

HEATH TOWN UNITED F.C.

Staff of the Joseph Evans Culwell Works in the late 1930s. This is the fitting and machinery shop where small pumps of up to three tons were made. The factory closed just after the Second World War but a large part of the Culwell Works still remains, split into smaller industrial units. Back row, left to right: Bill Martin, -?-, Phillip Tombs, Alf Mason, Bill Gibson, Jack Reynolds, Mr Rogers, Les Tombs, -?-, -?-, -?-, -?-, -?-. Second row: Joe Martin, Jack Williams, Mr James, -?-, Mr Turner, Alec Rowe, Jim Priest, Reg Brown, Ralph Bason, -?-, Mr Mansell, Mr Smith. Third row: Alf Crook, Charlie Lucas, -?-, Ernie Smith (foreman), Charlie Sackville, Mr Burton, Mr Marlow, -?-, -?-. Front row: Mr Pitt, Stanley George, -?-, -?-, -?-, -?-, -?-, Stan Jones, George Sant.

Opposite above: The Swan Inn, Heath Town, was on the corner of Church Street and Wednesfield Road. The landlord James Joyce stands in the doorway in the mid-1950s. The Swan was demolished in 1961.

Opposite below: A charabanc of Heath Town residents, ready to start on an outing from in front of a barber's shop.

The Boys' Brigade of Heath Town Congregational church at camp in Buildwas during the mid-1930s. Back row, first left is Arthur Ward and extreme right is Arthur Perry. Front row, left to right: Lionel Hughes, Phillip Tolley, Edward Lewis, -?-, Robert Anderson, -?-, Stanley Thickbroom.

The Girl's Life Brigade of Heath Town Congregational church at camp in Derby in 1937. Left to right: Connie Jones, ? Wagstaffe, Lilian Hughes, Ruth ?, Patricia Gutteridge, -?-.

The Red Lion Hotel, Church Street, Heath Town.

A Heath Town wedding party in 1928. Back row, left to right: Walter Jones, Uvedale Jones, -?-, Mrs Harriett Jones, -?-, Doris Wilkes (slightly forward), -?-, -?-, -?-, -?-. Front row, second left is Jessie Pace and in the middle is Lily Jones.

The twenty-first birthday gathering of Jean McGann (later Jean Mason) at Causeway Lake school in Alma Street, Heath Town, in 1946. Jean is in the front row behind the little girl. She was in the ATS but was allowed home on leave for her birthday. Her family lived in Raymond Terrace, Jones Avenue, and most of the people came from this area.

Opposite above: The Star Hotel on Wolverhampton Road, Heath Town, in November 1947. Cross Street runs alongside to the left. It was demolished with the rest of the area in the 1960s.

Opposite below: A children's New Year party inside the Star Hotel in 1952. There was a Punch and Judy show for the 150 children, each of which had a present courtesy of Mrs Brown the landlady.

An aerial view of, and around, New Cross Hospital between the World Wars. Most of the hospital buildings in evidence are former workhouses. The fields surrounding the hospital have now largely been filled with new hospital buildings. In the foreground is Heath Town Park, with Wednesfield Road and the Wyrley and Essington Canal to the right. Prestwood Road is on the extreme left, running past Heath Park school.

Opposite above: The Royal Ancient Order of the Buffaloes from Heath Town Lodge at a dinner in the Star Inn on 5 April 1952. In total, 104 people were present.

Oposite below: The Travellers Athletic Football Club in 1952. They played in the Seventh Division of the Wolverhampton League and were based at the Travellers Rest in Wolverhampton Road, Heath Town, a pub that was demolished in 1962. It was replaced by a new building at the end of Woden Road which is now also closed.

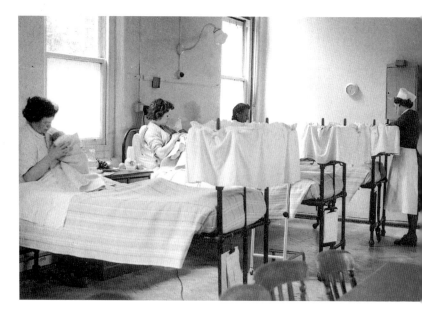

An aerial view of the hospital buildings, c. 1969. Looking in the direction of Bowman's Harbour, the new maternity block is being built in the background, with further construction work in the foreground.

The retirement of New Cross Hospital's matron, Miss Cain, in 1952. She is seated in the centre and to her right is the medical superintendent, Dr Lee. The group is outside the doctor's residence and includes doctors, staff ward sisters, nursing administration staff, the pharmacist and the hospital secretary. One of the ribbons worn by Miss Cain is the Dutch Orange Order awarded in recognition of the part played by New Cross in treating over 2,000 Dutch servicemen and sailors during the Second World War.

The maternity ward at New Cross before the new block was built in the late 1960s. New Cross Hospital is now the first part of Wolverhampton that many newborn babies see.

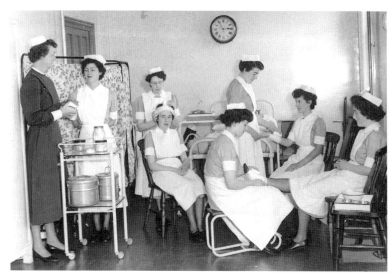

Student nurses undergoing training in the late 1950s. They are practising the application of dressings to head, hands and feet.

Student nurses relax outside their accommodation block at New Cross.

A class at Woden Road junior school, c. 1959. The teacher is Miss Tegwyn Morton (later Mrs Jackson).

The Crown Inn, Wolverhampton Road, New Cross, around 1965.

The vast new Heath Town housing estate under construction during June 1969.
The first part of the dual carriageway was later extended to the Springfield Road
junction, which can be seen in the distance. The council purchased 6,097 acres
to build over 600 dwellings, including 3 tower blocks. This photograph was taken
from Campion House and shows Alder House on the right. The short terrace of
houses and shops, and St Barnabas' church next door, are the only parts of the
old Heath Town to survive.

A view from Campion House towards the Deansfield area with Manders' Paints & Inks factory just beyond the block of flats. The factory moved to this site between 1926 and 1939 from its St John Street base.

A group of Mander Bros' staff who had met a production target in the 1960s. Back row, first left is Arthur Breakwell, fifth left is Ken Hall and sixth left is Jack Whitehouse. Second row from the front, extreme left is Arthur Eagle, second left is Charles Roberts, fourth right is George Cox and third right is Bob Knight. Front row, third left is Dennis Corfield.

The teaching staff at Woden Road school in the 1970s.

The new school built within the Heath Town housing estate was first occupied by St Stephen's primary school, until someone realized that they had moved outside the parish, thus making the school's title a misnomer. After they moved to the vacated Woden Road school buildings a new school called Long Ley was established here.

A class at St Stephen's school while they were still in the new Heath Town estate.

The netball team at St Stephen's school, before the building had become Long Ley school.

An aerial view of New Cross Hospital in the 1970s showing a great deal of building since the picture on p. 25. A new St Patrick's Roman Catholic school has been built on the edge of Heath Town Park in the foreground, replacing the one in Springfield. Extensive building has since gone ahead on the New Cross site, not least so that Wolverhampton's Royal Hospital could close and all hospital services could be concentrated on one site.

Opposite above: A view from Campion House showing the Heath Town baths to the left, Holy Trinity school just beyond and the bowling green alongside. In the background is Heath Town Park and New Cross Hospital.

Opposite below: The Wolverhampton company, Sir Alfred MacAlpine & Sons Ltd, building the new maternity block at New Cross Hospital during 1971. The building with the clock tower in the background is the old administrative building of Wolverhampton Workhouse.

Woden Road primary school football team, winners of the Dunstall League for the 1970-71 season.

Woden Road netball team, winners of the 'A' League in 1975-76.

Woden Road primary school chess team in 1971-72, winners of the Staley Chess Trophy.

Children from St Stephen's primary school, after the school had moved to the Woden Road buildings in 1979.

A view from Campion House looking towards Fallings Park, with Guy Motors' factory in the distance on the right. In the foreground is Station Road and the site of Wolverhampton's first station, Wednesfield Heath. Station Road splits into Powell Street to the left and Leslie Road to the right. The edge of the former Culwell Works can just be seen on the extreme left.

A view of the Heath Town estate from the Wednesfield goods depot yard in 1987. The spire of Holy Trinity church can just be seen on the skyline to the left. The goods yard has now had the giant automated Post Office sorting office built upon it.

Two

Park Village

At the turn of the century there was a garden suburb movement sweeping the country as a reaction to the closely packed streets of terraced houses which dominated many towns. The likes of Welwyn Garden City and Hemel Hempstead were products of a desire to give housing more room and to give residents their own gardens. In Wolverhampton, Sir Arthur Paget of the Old Fallings estate sponsored the establishment of just such a suburb on Fallings Park in a development that became known as Park Village.

Turf was cut for the first seven houses in 1907 and in September the following year a Model Housing Exhibition was opened, with houses built in competition by various local architects. By 1915 seventy-five houses had been completed in the development, but the First World War then put an end to the project. When house building resumed between the World Wars, the Park Village area was engulfed by expansion in Wolverhampton, Heath Town and Wednesfield. The area, which had essentially been a village surrounded on most sides by farmland, became an ill-defined suburb situated around Cannock Road.

The ceremony of the cutting of the first turf for the initial seven houses in Park Village, on 13 July 1907, performed by Lady Muriel and Sir Arthur Paget. Seated at the front are Councillor Coley of Heath Town UDC, Alderman Berrington, Lady Muriel Paget, The Mayor of Dudley, Councillor Bantock, ex-Mayor of Wolverhampton, Sir John Dickson-Poyndor MP. Standing behind the Union Jack is Sir Arthur Paget.

The opening of the Model Housing Exhibition at Park Village on 9 July 1908. The carriages were provided by Chubb's and Sir George Chubb was amongst the visiting party, having just laid the foundation stone for the new Chubb factory in Springfield.

Some of the many dignitaries gathered for the exhibition, including Viscount Wolverhampton. The village-like atmosphere was enhanced by imported maypole and morris dancers.

The crowd listen to the Lord Bishop of Lichfield carry out the opening ceremony. The houses in the background were in Victoria Road.

A gentleman cutting hay in the fields behind Victoria Road after the opening ceremonies were over. Park Village was largely surrounded by farmland at the time.

One of the houses built in Park Village for Mr Matthews who is in the garden with his wife, daughter and dog. The house cost £270 and later became 224 Bushbury Road. It remains there today but has had a large extension built on the side.

The Fallings Park Stores was owned by Blakemores Ltd, a company that was established in 1867 which had a chain of grocery stores in the town, but has now become a wholesaler. This shop was in Victoria Road, Park Village, during the 1920s and has since gone through several changes of ownership.

The Golden Wedding anniversary of Uvedale and Harriett Jones, with their six sons at the rear of their house in Prestwood Road in 1931. Left to right: Sidney, Clifford, Uvedale (junior), Walter, Albert, Uvedale (senior), Tom and, seated, Mrs Jones. Uvedale (senior) was formerly the head gardener at Hilton Park. A seventh son was killed during the First World War.

Bushbury Road, Park Village, before the First World War. Bushbury Road, in addition to Deans Road and Church Road in Heath Town, lay on the line of the ancient Worcester to Stafford road which ran along the Bushbury ridge.

The old Waggon and Horses on Cannock Road, which has now been replaced by a much newer building. This Banks' pub lay almost opposite a Butler's pub with the slightly more upmarket name of the Coach and Horses.

Cannock Road, running into Park Village, before the First World War. Park Village school is on the left. The houses beyond the school are no longer there, but those opposite remain.

Charles Wallbank sits in his 1914 Humber 3,458cc four-cylinder racing car behind his house, Glenmore, which was 144 Cannock Road. He found the car at Folkestone in 1925 and won a race at Brooklands in 1929. Up the steps in the background was the loft where he bred lop-eared rabbits.

This view of Victoria Road, Park Village, was taken from outside the Fallings Park Stores before the First World War.

Reg Brazier outside his home at 35 Crowther Street (off Nine Elms Lane), around 1909. He later became an 'iron roaster' and a foreman at the Chillington Tool Co., and was known locally as 'Posh' Brazier.

Harriet Jones stands outside her house in Prestwood Road, Park Village, in the 1930s. Until 1923 her husband, Uvedale, had been the head gardener at Hilton Park, Shareshill, the home of the Vernon family.

Left: A council election handout for John Lewis, a metal box and trunk manufacturer of Heath Town, who lived at 28 Prestwood Road. He was the Mayor of Wolverhampton from 1931 to 1932 but died while in office on 25 February 1932.

Below: Four views of the Prestwood Arms Hotel in Prestwood Road, showing they had their own brewery, as well as pleasure gardens and a bowling green for the amusement of customers.

A Christmas party for the local children at the Squirrel Inn, Bushbury Road, in 1951. This pub was demolished in 1960 and The Great Horse built on the site.

Park Village football team for the 1945-46 season, when they were winners of the Sir Robert Bird Cup. The team used the clubroom at the Park Inn as their base. The elderly man on the extreme left is Councillor Sam Tatton and the tall man just behind him is Walter Weaver.

Three

Springfield

In mid-Victorian times the boundary of east Wolverhampton was marked by the adjacent railway lines which ran into High Level and Low Level Station, and the parallel canal. Beyond these formidable barriers were the fields of Grimstone Farm on Cannock Road, which were known for their high water-table. The ancient Cul Well lay in the area and Smestow Brook had its beginnings there. When William Butler, who had built a successful brewing business in Priestfield, decided to expand he chose the Springfield area to build his new brewery because of the abundant water supply and the adjacent railway. Brewing began at the new location in 1874.

The cluster of terraced houses that sprang up around the brewery had been part of Wolverhampton's first attempts at planned housing development. St Stephen's church was built on Grimstone Street in the shadow of Springfield Brewery. When St Stephen's school took over the whole of the site, a new church was built nearby on Hilton Street. Housing spread out towards Heath Town and a secondary school was built on Springfield Road as the fields of Grimstone Farm finally disappeared.

When Chubb Locks and Safes needed to build a new factory to replace the one on Broad Street in the town centre, they chose the last few fields in Springfield, right up against the boundary of Heath Town. They became the third major employer of the tight little community after the railways and Butler's.

Mr Jack Coxshall with his horse Tommy outside Butler's Brewery, Cambridge Street, in 1946. He had gone to work for Butler's after being a drayman with Russell's Brewery on the other side of the railways. Russell's had been taken over by Butler's in 1927.

The arrival of the Duke and Duchess of York at Low Level Station in 1900.

The arrival of Colonel A. Thorneycroft inside Low Level Station in 1900. The colonel is on the left of the Mayor of Wolverhampton, the gentleman with the chain.

William Butler, founder of the Springfield Brewery, with some of his friends on a shooting party, around 1888. Back row, left to right: Mr Joynson the head keeper, Mr William Butler, Mr William Bruford, 'Mr Bruford's man'. Front row: the keeper's son, Mr Reynolds (an innkeeper), Mr Butler's coachman.

One of Butler's earliest lorries, a steam-powered machine with trailer. It carries one of Wolverhampton's earliest number plates DA 36. The member of the crew standing by the front wheel was named Rogers.

This steam-powered lorry was owned by Chubb Safes who were established in London by 1846, but did not move to their Springfield site until after 1908. Chubb Locks was already established in Wolverhampton at their Broad Street factory.

A Chubb thirty ton strong-room door for the Prudential Assurance leaving the Springfield factory on a L.M.S. Scammell articulated low-loader.

Harry Withers Chubb, one of the grandsons of the founder of the firm, Charles Chubb, standing in front of a strong-room door and gate manufactured by the company.

Butler's Brewery staff at their Queen Street shop in 1905.

St Stephen's church junior club football team were winners of the Wolverhampton Club League in 1906 and 1907. Back row, extreme left is Revd Tunnadine.

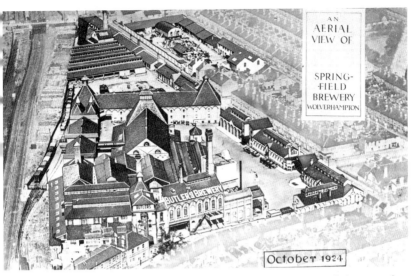

An aerial view of William Butler's Springfield Brewery in 1924. It remains much the same today, though most of the terraced houses which surrounded it at the time have now gone.

Butler's drays at Brewood Show in the 1930s. Reg Brazier is the driver of No. 108.

Butler's football team outside the Springfield Road sports ground in the 1920s. Middle row, third right is Clarence Williamson and extreme right is Billy Clark. Front row, extreme left is Howard Broadfield and second left is Mr Townsend.

Outside the Springfield Brewery is one of Butler's floats, which used to visit Stafford Show annually between the World Wars. It represents one of Butler's pubs, the Greyhound and Punchbowl, formerly the Stow Heath Manor House. Top right is Howard Broadfield who is dressed as 'Sarah Lamp'.

Butler's drivers, known as the Forwarding Department, around 1932. Back row, second right is Tommy Griffiths. Middle row, extreme left is Billy Gardner and third left is Howard Broadfield. Howard's lorry was No. 9 in the right background.

The loading bank in Springfield Brewery yard, with a mixture of horse-drawn and motorised transport, around 1938. In the centre of the cobbled yard is the First World War memorial to the local men who died.

The St Stephen's Operatic Society production of the *Pirates of Penzance* in Easter 1937. The society was based at St Stephen's church in Hilton Street.

Opposite above: St Stephen's school cricket team in 1939. St Stephen's opened in Springfield Road in 1881 but moved into the Grimstone Street church buildings in 1898. By 1914 the whole school was on the site, lying in the shadow of Springfield Brewery.

Opposite below: A line-up of Butler's Brewery vehicles in Cambridge Street, ready for the May Day parade in 1950. The pupils at St Stephen's school, at the end of the street, were allowed time off each year to watch the parade.

No. 1047 Squadron, Air Training Corps, at Springfield Road school in 1942. The cups were for a foot drill contest. On the second row from the back, second from the left is Les Broadfield.

Opposite above: The Springfield Road secondary school football team remained unbeaten during the 1934-35 season. The captain, holding the shield, is George Lawrence.

Opposite below: The apprentice's dinner at Springfield Brewery in 1940. On the extreme left is the newly qualified cooper, Reg Wainwright and, on the extreme right, his father Sam 'Pop' Wainwright, who also worked at Butler's.

Above left: A group gathered around the barrel organ which provided music for the Beacon Street VE Day street party. Left to right: Mr Cox (with striped tie), Mr Adams who kept a fish and chip shop, Jack Chappell, -?-, Mr Francis, Mrs Adams, Mrs Helliwell, Mr Payne.

Above right: The party obviously developed into a knees-up! The lady in the soldier's hat and tunic is Elsie Anne Cartwright whose husband, Gordon, served with the Signals in North Africa, France, Italy and Germany.

Opposite above: Ladies gathered for the Beacon Street VE Day street party, with Cannock Road stretching into the distance. Beacon Street does not exist any more as it was demolished to make way for new housing.

Opposite below: Beacon Street children tuck into the food at the Beacon Street party for VE Day in 1945. The first two on the left are Teresa Evans and John Evans.

St Stephen's school in Grimstone Street with Springfield Brewery behind. In 1914, the whole school had been concentrated in this one building, which included St Stephen's church before it moved to a new site in Hilton Street.

Teachers from St Stephen's school in 1953. Back row, left to right: Joan Clinton, Keith Ball, Margaret Morton, Maisie Smith. Front row: Margery Wedge, Ruth Marsh (deputy head), Reg Warton (head teacher), Pat Hughes, Effie Wood. Margaret Morton had been sent, by her father, to St Stephen's for a short period before training to be a teacher. He thought that it would put her off teaching as he wanted her to become a doctor. The ruse failed, however, as she became a teacher for the next forty years!

St Stephen's netball team for the 1957-58 season.

A group of children pose in St Stephen's playground, ready to perform *Alice through the Looking Glass*. The bakery in Water Street is behind.

Above: A 1953 Coronation party held in a courtyard at the back of the houses in Grimstone Street. The courtyard stretched from the Lamp Tavern to the hairdresser's next door.

Left: Twins David and Diane Roberts cutting the cake for the Coronation celebrations at St Stephen's school in 1953. The proud lady behind is their grandmother Mrs Davies.

A general view of the Coronation Day party held at St Stephen's school.

Bill Beards holds his horse, Topper, during May Day at the brewery. The celebrations were an annual event in the Springfield area when local people could visit and schoolchildren, who got the day off, were given free pop and crisps. The war memorial behind had now been raised in height to add the names of those who died in the Second World War.

Butler's fire crew put on a demonstration as part of the May Day celebrations in 1957.

A Westland Widgeon helicopter on the cricket ground near the Springfield Road allotments. It had come to take copies of the *Sporting Star* to Wembley for selling to Wolves fans coming out of the FA Cup final on 7 May 1960. The people gathered around are from Springfield Road and the clubhouse, where they had been watching the Wolves' win on television.

A class at St Stephen's in the early 1970s. In 1971 the school had moved to a new building on the Heath Town estate, but Grimstone Street remained open as a one-class annexe. By 1975, numbers had risen to 556 and the school was full once again.

The cooperage at Butler's Brewery, around 1960. From left to right: Ted Lewis, Mick Barnes (apprentice cooper), Tony Purchase.

The beginning of the apprentice initiation ceremony for Mick Barnes who is being lowered into a barrel by Ted Lewis (left) and Tom Barnes. Extreme right is Dick Birch, the head cooper.

The barrel, having been filled with soot, sawdust, yeasty water and stale beer, is rolled down the cobbled yard with Mick inside.

Mick is tipped from the barrel at the end of his ordeal. Those present are, from left to right: Reg Wainwright, Tom Barnes, Dick Birch (slightly hidden), -?-, J.P. Mullard, -?-. Reg might be smiling because he was remembering his own such initiation, just before the apprentices' dinner shown on p. 60.

Change arrives at Butler's with steel barrels making the skill of the cooper redundant. Former cooper Ted Lewis (right) shows the Bishop of Wolverhampton how the new kegs are filled.

Springfield United football team from the 1948-49 season. They represented the Springfield Working Men's Club and played on Fowler's playing fields. Back row, left to right: G. Blower, J. Lees, J. Danno, E. Cox, A. Rozier, J. Heritage, G. Pearcey. Middle row: R. Sands, H. Williams, W. Horton, Mrs A. Pearcey, E. Franks, B. Horton. G. Harris, Front row: G. Bott, K. Lewin.

The delivery of a large vessel to the Springfield Brewery. The name W. Butler disappeared from above the gate in 1964 after the business had been taken over by Mitchell & Butler's of Birmingham in 1961.

This 1950s view of Grimstone Street was taken from high in the brewery. The Lamp Tavern can be seen bottom right. Only the detached house in front of the van remains today, all the rest have been replaced by industrial units.

An aerial view of Springfield, around 1960, with the land owned by the brewery outlined. The housing in the foreground has largely been cleared, but at the bottom right of the picture St Patrick's school still remains. On the right the terraced houses in Cambridge Street and Beacon Street still remain. The two railways and the canal, which cut off Springfield from the town centre, can all be seen.

Wednesfield Road goods depot in the early 1960s. This had originally been part of the Midland Railway, though it was adjacent to the Great Western Railway's Low Level Station.

The Wednesfield Road goods depot site became redundant in the early 1990s. Though the depot was first linked with heritage schemes centred on the Low Level Station (which is a listed building), it was demolished in 1996 and a new Post Office sorting centre was built on the site.

A Castle Class locomotive with carriages leaves Low Level for Birmingham in 1963. The Sun Street bridge, which has now been demolished, is in the background. Once the old LMS High Level line had been electrified, passenger services from Low Level to Snow Hill were allowed to decrease.

A Castle Class locomotive approaches Low Level with a down express in 1963. Wolverhampton and Birchley Rolling Mills are in the background.

Engine No. 5063, *Earl Baldwin*, stands in the carriage shed at the back of Low Level Station in 1963.

Low Level Station, when it was a parcel depot, in 1973. The station closed in 1981 and has slowly become derelict as various heritage schemes have come and gone. The station and the listed Springfield Brewery site, which is only yards away, offer a great opportunity for heritage-based development.

Sports Day at Woden primary school on the playing fields behind St Stephen's church, in the 1970s. Woden Road school, Heath Town, moved to the old Springfield Road secondary school buildings in 1976, which allowed the old Woden Road buildings to be occupied by St Stephen's school. The school was found to be outside the parish of St Stephen's when it moved to the buildings in Heath Town.

Woden primary school's boys rounders team were winners of the Heath Town League in 1983.

One of the last classes at St Stephen's Grimstone Street annexe in the mid-1970s. When the main school moved to the Woden Road buildings in 1979, Grimstone Street was closed and became a community centre. Hanish Patel is the teacher on the left.

This aerial view of Cannock Road Garages Ltd in 1989 shows the Coach and Horses pub on the right and Hilton Street in the background. This was the site of Grimstone Farm, the last in the area. The pub has now been demolished and the garage has expanded to cover the whole of this triangle of land.

Part of the huge Chubb factory on Wednesfield Road. It was often thought that the factory was in Heath Town, but it was in fact entirely within Springfield.

The footbridge over the closed GWR railway line, with Springfield Brewery beyond. The steps to this bridge from Grimstone Street were known as 'The Nineteen Steps', though there were only eighteen. A drainage channel at the bottom used to form a slight extra step, but this is now covered over with asphalt. Before the Second World War, a Japanese couple, Mr and Mrs Watabiki, kept a fish and chip shop at the foot of the steps. Mr Watabiki went to work in a factory during the war, but his family still live in the town.

Four

Stafford Street to Broad Street

The route to Heath Town and Springfield starts at Broad Street (formerly Canal Street) in the town centre and then beyond the railways becomes Wednesfield Road. The route to Fallings Park and the northern part of Heath Town starts as Stafford Street before turning off to Cannock Road. Between Broad Street, Stafford Street and the Birmingham canal there used to be a small area of terraced housing that mirrored Springfield on the other side of the railway. This area was usually called Carribbee Island, or sometimes St Mary's, and included its own brewery for a while. Russell's was located in Great Western Street but it was taken over by Butler's and closed in 1927. The main company in the area became Carver's, a sawmill and timber yard, which became the main supplier of building materials in Wolverhampton. Carver's had occupied the former Herbert Street goods depot.

Attracted, perhaps, by St Patrick's Catholic church, the area became known for the concentration of Irish families. The housing, which was some of the worst in Wolverhampton, was largely cleared away in the 1950s. None of the housing remains as the ring road sliced through it in the 1970s. In the 1960s and 1970s, the area was known for the famous Lafayette which was one of the best nightclubs in Wolverhampton. Today the Canal Club has assumed its mantle.

The Broad Street and Stafford Street junction in June 1975. Broad Street goes straight on, under the railway where a train can just be seen, and towards the distant Heath Town flats. Stafford Street goes to the left.

A Lorain system tram in Lichfield Street around the turn of the century. It is passing the Grand Theatre on the left, where *When Knights Were Bold* is playing. In the background Prince's Square marks the start of Stafford Street.

Employees of T. Russell's Great Western Street brewery just before the First World War. On the dray the man with his arms folded is Mr Titley.

Mary Coxshall, whose husband Jack worked for Russell's Brewery, sits on the dray horse, called Polly Perkins, in the brewery yard in the 1920s.

The Warwick Arms, on the corner of St Mary's Terrace and Little's Lane, when Joseph Henry Price was the licensee. It was a pub frequently used by the Irish community in Carribbee Island.

The Crown Street depot of Wright Bros Ltd, a large transport company. The Wright family now operates the Cannock Road garage not far away.

A Wright Bros articulated truck carrying the 1,000hp Sunbeam, the first car in the world to exceed 200mph. It is ready to take part in a Cavalcade of Transport through the streets of Wolverhampton.

Broad Street in October 1973 shortly before the buildings up to Westbury Street (the road off to the right) were demolished.

The old Olympia Cinema in Thornley Street soon after its closure. The building in the distance became the Lafayette Club and, in more recent times, the Rubicon casino.

No. 70012, *John of Gaunt*, leaving for London from Wolverhampton High Level Station in 1963. The station roof was removed during the electrification of the line in 1967. The station is on the other side of Broad Street from Carribee Island, and trains coming from the north pass along its eastern side.

Opposite above: St Patrick's church on Little's Lane opened in 1867. It is shown here in the 1960s when much of the surrounding housing had already been removed. The church has now been demolished and replaced by a new St Patrick's in Heath Town.

Opposite below: The last wedding to take place inside the old St Patrick's church before it was demolished.

Broad Street bridge, which goes over the canal, in October 1973. British Waterways' Broad Street depot has now become the Canal Club. The Union Inn on the other side of the road was demolished to allow widening of the road when the ring road was built.

A Bailey bridge was installed over the canal to allow the demolition of the old Broad Street structure in July 1975. Chubb Locks is on the left, and the building with a tower to the right is now a nightclub.

The old and the new in January 1976. The old Broad Street bridge is to the left and the new concrete one is to the right. The diversion to the canal and a temporary coffer-dam are also visible. The stonework of the old bridge was numbered so that it could be rebuilt in the Black Country Museum.

Broad Street Basin after it had been redeveloped. The lock-keeper's cottages are in the background and the Lock Street bridge is beyond. The bridge leads to the route for the 'Nineteen Steps' and Springfield.

Children from Woden primary school, Springfield Road, walk underneath Broad Street bridge in 1984. By this time the original bridge had been re-erected in the Black Country Museum.

This view of Long Street was taken in 1974 before the cobbles had been covered with a layer of asphalt. Long Street runs from Broad Street to Fryer Street.

A 1947 Sunbeam trolleybus in Stafford Street in 1963. It is on the No. 9 route to Amos Lane in Fallings Park.

The bottom end of Fryer Street in 1973. All of the buildings in this photograph have since been demolished, and the road is now the start of the route to Wolverhampton Station. H.R.D. Motorcycles used to have a factory on Fryer Street, where H.R. Davies produced his winning motorbikes for the TT Isle of Man event.

St Mary Street in 1973, just before it was demolished to make way for the Westbury Street car park. The YMCA is directly ahead.

A special train for Carlisle pulled by No. 46251, *City of Nottingham*, arriving at High Level Station in 1964. The station was completely rebuilt for electrification with fine views of Heath Town and beyond, but rather less protection from the weather for waiting passengers.

Five

Fallings Park

The suburb of Fallings Park mainly lies on the Old Fallings estate of the Gough family, which was later taken over by the Pagets. When the Paget family encouraged the building of a garden suburb on the estate before the First World War, construction was largely confined to the Park Village area. Large industrial companies had already moved into Park Lane including Guy Motors and the Efandem battery factory. After the First World War, the industrialisation of that area continued with the arrival of Henry Meadows, Ever Ready and the car companies Star and Clyno, though their stay proved to be short-lived. The rest of the Fallings Park area was redeveloped in a style typical of the 1920s and 1930s, completely engulfing Park Village. The famous names of Park Lane, Guy Motors, Henry Meadows and Ever Ready closed down in the changing industrial times of the 1980s and smaller companies replaced them.

This view of Bickford Road, Fallings Park, between the World Wars illustrates the garden suburb nature of the area. Bickford Road, off Victoria Road in the Park Village area, was typical of many of the surrounding streets.

FLORENCE NIGHTINGALE

TO
BLIGH

The works and office staff of Guy Motors, around 1923. Back row, first left is Mr Holmes, fifth left is Jim Stanley and first from the right is Mr Piper the timekeeper. Fourth row, first left is Fred Crump the Commissioner, second left is Horace Amos and sixth right is Mr Cadwallader with a monocle. Third row, first left is Lawrence Goring, second left is Harry Court, third left is Frank Harman, fifth left is Mr Allen and sixth left is Miss Heighway. Second row, first left is Tony Guy the brother of Sidney Guy and the Sales Director, and first right is Sam Massey the Personnel Manager and owner of a greengrocer's in Whitmore Reans.

Opposite above: A float for the Victory Parade outside the Guy Motors' factory in 1919. It has been made to look like the hospital ship *Florence Nightingale* and has local children aboard. In the centre, the larger boy with his arm in a sling is Jim Stanley who had just joined the company straight from school.

Opposite below: Cannock Road, where it passes through Fallings Park. The children would not be able to play in the road today as it is now one of the main arterial routes out of the town.

Guy Motors when Park Lane was still not completely developed, around 1927. The second storey had not been built yet on the office block in front of the factory.

A Guy Promenade Runabout, around 1922. Usually known as a 'toast rack' for obvious reasons, they were popular at seaside resorts like Bournemouth and Rhyl. It is shown outside the Guy offices in Park Lane.

Britain's first six-wheeled double-decker bus (one of many Guy firsts) was handed over to Wolverhampton Council outside the Town Hall in 1926.

A Guy float with a nautical theme. The good ship *Humanity* with a banner that says 'All in the same boat'. It was crewed by local children, though the reason for the parade is not known.

A Guy six-wheel armoured car chassis in Park Lane around 1930. The gentleman behind the wheel is W.E. Bullock, a Guy director. These vehicles were extensively used in India. To the left is the Ever Ready factory (previously Efandem) and on the right the second storey of the Guy offices is being built.

Guy six-wheel trucks in production on 20 November 1928. They were the first such vehicles produced in Britain and both rear axles were driven. They were used by the Army as gun tractors, G.S. wagons and field workshops.

The Golden Lion pub in Cannock Road, Fallings Park, opened on 6 February 1935, and is shown here in July 1947.

Burns & Co. The Corn Stores, in Fallings Park. The firm had several other similar shops and their head office was in Willenhall.

Children from Old Fallings junior school on an outing to London on 13 May 1939.

The St Mary's school cricket team in the 1920s. The school was established in 1927 on 5,000 square yards of the Old Fallings estate, with the local Catholic community raising the necessary £479 9s 10d. The school was extended twice in 1936 and 1937. A new Catholic church, Our Lady of the Perpetual Succour, was built next door in 1934.

The Clifton cinema, Fallings Park, was the last in Wolverhampton to be built, in 1938. It was demolished in 1962 and replaced by a supermarket which has undergone a number of name changes: Fine Fare, Gateway and now Somerfield.

A large group of full-time female workers during the Second World War at Guy Motors. The factory had been turned over entirely to Government use in 1938 and their Ant and Quad-Ant military vehicles, the Guy light tank and a searchlight generator chassis were in full production.

The 10th Wolverhampton Sea Scouts were based in Newbridge Crescent. They are seen here on an elaborate float, built on an old Guy chassis, for National Savings Week at Guy's playing fields in 1945. Left to right: Ivor ?, ? Burton, Guy ? (in sou'wester), Peter Tatlow, scoutmaster and admiral Eric Williams, ? Roberts, ? Soulsby, -?-, Jim Male, Keith Ambler, Frank ?.

Opposite above: 'The Saving Graces' were five girls who sold savings stamps around the Guy factory on every Saturday morning during the Second World War. Their average was £300, but in the Wings for Victory week they sold an amazing £32,434. It is not known why they chose Scottish costume.

Oposite below: With so much of the wartime work being done inside, behind blackout curtains, Guy's felt their staff were not getting enough sun. This sun-ray lamp was installed so that workers could have a free session every week.

When the Springfield Brewery closed in 1991 the war memorial that had stood in the yard was brought to the Springfield Working Mens Club. It has now been moved to the Territorial Army headquarters in Fallings Park.

Left: A tank travels through Fallings Park around 8.30 a.m. Every Sunday morning in the 1950s, three Centurion tanks from the West Park Territorial Army Centre trundled along Cannock Road on their way to Cannock Chase.

Below: The Third Heath Town Scout Pipe Band marching along the Cannock Road through Fallings Park, *c.* 1950. They probably made as much noise as the tanks!

The Guy Motors' light vehicle assembly line, where Guy Vixen chassis are being assembled, soon after the Second World War.

The Fallings Park Youth Club football team in 1945. Their shirts were made of old blackout material that must have soaked up the sweat!

A netball match between the Fisher Bearings' team and boys from the Fallings Park Youth Club in 1948.

A Sunbeam trolleybus passing under the Cannock Road bridge on its way to Fallings Park in 1964. Guy Motors took over the Sunbeam trolleybus business and amalgamated it with its own. All electric buses were Sunbeams while motorised buses were Guys.

The St Mary's school football team in the 1950-51 season.

The St Mary's school netball team from the same year.

Teaching staff at St Mary's in the 1950s.

Sports Day at St Mary's in the 1950s with the Church of the Perpetual Succour behind. This three-legged race has already produced a couple of fallers and two young contestants who are no longer tied together.

Workers leaving the Ever Ready factory in Park Lane. The site was first occupied by the battery maker Efandem who had moved from Birmingham in 1911. The company's name derived from the initials of the two directors, F. and M. They fell into serious financial difficulties in 1925 and the business was taken over by Ever Ready.

Potential African distributors receive instructions on Ever Ready's saucepan radio in the 1950s. A cheap, sturdy model for Third World markets, the prototype was actually made in a saucepan!

Part of the radio production area at Ever Ready. The firm's workforce reached a peak of 3,000 employees. The battery side of the business was usually still known as the Efandem.

Ever Ready workers on a trip to Wolverhampton Airport where they sampled a Don Everall Aviation DC-3 airliner.

The new bus workshop at Guy Motors in 1952. An especially high building had to be constructed to take the double-decker line.

The retirement presentation of Don Shipley at Guy Motors in July 1953. Those watching include Kenneth James, Reg Biston, Dennis Bills, Harry Field, Jack Fairfield, Harry Taylor and Matt Davies. They are standing alongside a Guy Ant that is partly visible on the left.

Sunbeam trolleybuses await disposal outside the depot in 1963. One of Guy's biggest customers for buses was the Wolverhampton Corporation as their Park Lane bus depot was opposite the factory. Guy's offices can be seen in the background on the left.

Guy Arab diesel buses alongside the Park Lane bus depot in the 1970s. A trolleybus bracket survives overhead as a reminder of a different era.

Left: Guy drawing office staff in front of a Guy coach that belongs to Don Everall Ltd. They are on their way to the MIRA test track where they tested the vehicle at high speed with a full load of passengers. Third from the right, wearing the glasses is Ray Simpson.

Below: A Guy 'Big J' recovery vehicle in Park Lane, ready for delivery to Guy's Scottish service depot.

Guy apprentices outside the factory in 1947. Standing, left to right: Rex Bellamy, Mick Maplow, Jeff Thomas, Cyril Brown, David Griffiths, Norman Jones, Stan Bachelor, Cedric Lewis, Johnny Adams, Ted Handford, John Dudley, Mr Yates, Don Shepherd, John Barnett, Warwick Pearson. Sitting: Jeff Beach, John Young, Derek Pickering, Walter Gwilliam, John Freeman, Wilf Palfreyman.

A large percentage of the Guy workforce surrounds the 5,000th Guy 'Big J' truck in August 1969. By this time, Guy Motors had been taken over, first by Jaguar, and then by British Leyland. The company was closed in 1982 despite having a full order book and being the only division of British Leyland, apart from Land Rover, to make a profit.

The Union of Catholic Mothers follow children from St Mary's school to the neighbouring Church of the Perpetual Succour for their first communion.

A very attentive class of juniors at St Mary's school.

Above and below: Girls and boys from classes at St Mary's school posed for group photographs before they attended their first communion.

A reunion of Ever Ready staff in 1996. The company was shut down in the spring of 1980 after the workforce had been steadily reduced to 1,100. Falling demand for products such as cycle lamp batteries was blamed for the factory's demise. The reunion was organized by Trevor and June Ridgway. Trevor is kneeling at the front and June is second left in the middle row.

Opposite above: Fire engines outside Fallings Park fire station in the late 1980s. The station opened in 1960 to serve the northern part of Wolverhampton. Fallings Park now also looks after a number of vintage fire vehicles.

Opposite below: St Mary's school football team for the 1968-69 season.

Above: Guy Motors drawing office on Park Lane in 1984. This is the only part of the Guy Motors factory that still survives; the rest was demolished to make way for smaller industrial units.

Left: The Guy Motors site in 1984 as demolition takes place. The firm was the last of a number of major companies in the Fallings Park area to disappear including Ever Ready, Henry Meadows, Star Cars, Clyno Cars and A.B. Coupler.

Six

Wood End

In the Middle Ages, when much of the area covered by this book was woodland, various clearings were cut in the forest. The hamlet of Wood End was one of these. Part of Wednesfield parish, the area remained strictly agricultural well into the twentieth century. As housing began to spread out from Wolverhampton, Heath Town and Wednesfield, Wood End was engulfed.

   The limits of expansion were Wood End Road and Linthouse Lane where the boundary of Wednesfield (part of Wolverhampton from 1966) was established. When the West Midlands was created this line became the county boundary. Beyond, in the Staffordshire fields between Blackhalve Lane and Kitchen Lane, Alan Cobham used to bring his flying circus in the 1930s. Apart from this brief excitement, however, Wood End was more of a quiet residential suburb.

At the turn of the century this was a typical scene in the Wood End area: a reaping machine on Ashmore Farm at a time when farming was still very labour intensive.

Ashmore Farm with the remains of the medieval moat in the foreground.

A cottage in Blackhalve Lane before the turn of the century that is typical of the rural nature of the area around this time.

The Wood Hayes public house on 1 August 1957, the day that it opened. It could be found at the corner of Blackhalve Lane and Wood End Road, on the edge of Wolverhampton, with the Staffordshire county boundary just behind.

Oxley Football Club were based at the Wood Hayes pub. They are shown in the 1959-60 season when they were Wolverhampton Amateur League Premier Division champions, and also winners of the Charity Cup and the Sir Alfred Bird Cup.

Left: A small cottage in Ridge Lane by the crooked bridge over the Wyrley and Essington Canal. It was occupied in the 1950s by an elderly lady named Mrs Turner, who had to borrow drinking water as there was no supply to the cottage. She died in the 1960s and the cottage was soon demolished.

Below: Elves, fairies and woodland animals at Wood End primary school in 1944. The school had opened in 1938 to cater for the growing population of the suburb and had an initial roll of 272 pupils and 7 teachers.

Opposite above: A large production at Wood End primary school in the 1940s. The subject of the play once again appears to be based around the woodland, which is appropriate for a district that was created as a clearing in the forest.

Opposite below: The Wood End girl's netball team in 1947 with Mrs Wild, the teacher, at the back. The school's green and gold uniform had not yet been introduced. A notable former Wood End sportswoman of more recent years was Olympic javelin champion Tessa Sanderson.

The Wood End primary school football team of the 1950-51 season, in the days when 'boots' really meant boots. Second left on the back row is John Shannon, who was head teacher from 1946 to 1968.

A class group at Wood End in the 1950s; a rainy Thursday 16 November in an unknown year. Note that the one-third pints of milk still came in real glass bottles.

A class group at Wood End in 1965. The school was greatly expanded in 1961, with a new set of classrooms being built. Back row, from left to right: Andrew Gough, Robert Grindley, Dennis Bradnock, David ?, Vincent Adamski, Denise Holder, Julia Dickens. Third row: Peter Cossey, David Sanders, Ralph Webster, Ian Wollam, Derek Baker, Pamela Whitley, Martin Buckley, Ann Tyler, Susan Harley, Gene Baroninus, Pat Ward, Helen Dale, Rita Bullingham. Second row: Susan Tyler, Moira Crutchley, David Badger, Timothy Ball, Stephen Forward, Michael Jones, Valerie Garlick, Margaret Doherty, Angela Smith, Linda Turner. Front row: Rosamund Matthews, Margaret Nussey, Denise Hodgkiss, Lynda Baker, Penny Sandal, Hilary Parker.

The Wood End school football squad in the 1976-77 season. The head teacher on the left is Mr Blackhall and the teacher on the right is Tom Stockin.

March 1947 saw the country in the grips of one of the most vicious winters this century. These buses, which took miners to Hilton Main Colliery, were stranded in Essington Road and remained there for some time.

Acknowledgements

I have to thank a host of people for helping me with this book, all of which I hope are mentioned below. In particular there are several who have given me extensive assistance. John McNish let me borrow freely from his huge collection of Fallings Park photographs. David Clare's photographs of the inner suburbs of Wolverhampton in the 1970s yielded many of the Broad Street area. Both John Chappell and Richard Morgan were able to find me many photographs of the Springfield area, where they have always lived and worked. Once more Harry Blewitt's huge collection of Wolverhampton postcards yielded a number from the area covered by this book. Ken Hale's marvellous photographs of the days of steam once more proved him to be a railway enthusiast as well as a railwayman.

Others who need a mention are: Keith Ball, Mr A. Bates, Mrs Elsie Bradley, George Brazier, Mr A. Breakwell, Les Broadfield, Ray Brown, Gerry Cheese, Malcolm Eden, Mrs Dorothy Egan, Jim Evans, Harry Field, Neil Fox of New Cross Hospital, Mr Harmon of St Stephen's school, Ron Holmes, Mrs Tegwyn Jackson, Norman Jones, Mr P.A. Jones, Mrs Lewis, Mr J. Lewis, Bill Lockley, Jim Male, Mrs Jean Mason, Irene Millman, Ben Owen, Mrs R. Paterson, Trevor and June Ridgway, Mrs Roberts of St Mary's school, Mr H.S. Roberts, Andy Simpson, Ray Simpson, Roy Stallard, Jim Stanley, Kevin Summers, Mrs T. Taylor, Mrs Beryl Till, Mrs Tomkins, Mrs E. Turner, Mrs D. Watson, Mr H. Wiggins, Mr Wright of Cannock Road Garage, Janet Visser, Mr P. Prescott of Wood End primary school, John Barnett and, for the umpteenth time, Wendy Matthiason.